I love my hair!

by Maria Peevey
and Megan Weinerman

Illustrations by Kristin Kelly Colombano

SimplyShe™

Stewart, Tabori & Chang
New York

Conceived and created by SimplyShe™

With particular thanks to Jean Orlebeke for her amazing talent in working with us to design SimplyShe products. Thanks to Andrew Finkelman for letting us drink, spew, and parade like rock stars at his fabulous bar the Gin Joint. And, to the She's (and the one He of She), Alexis, Greg, Lisa, Michelle, and Virginia, thank you for your incredible loyalty and unwavering support in the larger vision which has helped make this a reality.

Published by
Stewart, Tabori & Chang
A Company of La Martinière Groupe
115 West 18th Street
New York, NY 10011

Export Sales to all countries except Canada,
France, and French-speaking Switzerland:
Thames & Hudson Ltd.
181A High Holborn
London WC1V 7QX
England

Canadian Distribution:
Canadian Manda Group
One Atlantic Avenue, Suite 105
Toronto, Ontario M6K 3E7
Canada

ISBN: 1-58479-254-X

Printed in China

10 9 8 7 6 5 4 3 2 1

Preface

Let's face it — most of us need to get real with ourselves and get real fast. Meaning, learn to like yourself because you're the only YOU you've got. Or you could go on forever {as many people do} trying to understand or lament the *Why's, What-Ifs, Maybes, If-Onlys, Shoulds, Coulds* and *Oughts*. But why do that when you don't have to? To make a change, what you really need is immediate support, direct praise, and useful guidance — INSTANTLY — at your fingertips. So start improving your life, your outlook, and your appearance by believing in yourself NOW. You'll be much happier, and you just might find that you actually like your hair, too! So what are you waiting for? Get started and read on — you're on your way to a new you.

Get Real

You love your hair.

Choosing Acceptance

Make peace with your hair by choosing to accept it. Start by picturing your hair as it was when you were a child. Remember how healthy and carefree it was pre-color, pre-blow dry, pre-flat-iron? Learning to accept something is no easy task, especially when it comes to your hair. But if you accept your hair, you may find that you can learn to love it, as it is — naturally.

Draw your hair

MY HAIR ACCEPTED AS IT IS

Releasing Expectations

Claim success for yourself by simply being Successful at Life. Start by making a set of *I Need a Flash!* cards. Get some index cards and on each one write a statement that speaks to you, such as:

I love life!

I am important because I am here!

I am smarter than my boss!

I am great in bed!

I've got it {and you can't have it}!

Remember, these are *your* flash cards, so anything goes! Then, whenever you need a lift give yourself a flash!

Clearing Obstacles

Rid yourself of unnecessary baggage. If something is unacceptable, draw a circle of acceptance around it. Just keep drawing more circles around each thing until nothing unacceptable is left uncircled. Watch how easy it is to accept something when you surround it instead of it surrounding you. You'll find that you *really* love circles. And it's good to love.

Start drawing

Everything you say is fascinating.

Awakening the Inner Voice

Get a journal. Title it *Everything I Say is Fascinating*. Write a journal entry every day. It can be anything. It can even be "I hate you, motherfucker." Or your "to-do" list. Then, when your journal is finished {and know that it's *your* decision when the journal is finished!} turn it into your own cool coffee table book—hard, glossy cover and all! Now everyone will tell you how great the book is. That means *you're* great because you wrote everything in it!

There is just something special about you.

Practicing Self-Worth

Finish these sentences:

A} I look really *great* in _____

_____

B} I feel exceptionally *good* when _____

_____

C} I excel *wildly* at _____

_____

D} I am better than *any* of you because _____

_____

E} You'll *all* be sorry that _____

_____

If you answered D and E seriously, you need to take a moment and look deep inside yourself! What do you see? Negative energy, that's what! Now go back to A and get positive. You must look great in *something!*

Your perception of reality is right on target.

Achieving Perspective

See things from a different point of view. Picture yourself rising into the air on a balloon. To gain height, you need to let go of some things. List three things or people you want to let go of so you can feel lighter:

1 } —————————————————————————————

2 } —————————————————————————————

3 } —————————————————————————————

Hint: People often weigh more than things.

Get Moving

You look attractive in anything you wear.

Banishing Blame

Make the mirror a happy place. Next time you find yourself in a dressing room, airplane bathroom, or anywhere you can see your fluorescent reflection, recite the three statements below. Keep reciting them for as long as necessary to remind yourself how beautiful your body really is:

1} My complexion is soft and smooth like a young flower, saturated with dew-drenched wholesomeness.

2} My breasts are magnificent to behold, like plump mountain peaks dominating the landscape with bold curves and natural beauty!

3} My stomach is flat as calm, glassy waters supporting all that is beneath its life-giving surface!

You make things happen

Actualizing Outcomes

1} Grab a pen and paper.

2} Go to the bathroom.

3} Close the door.

4} Write down one obstacle that you feel is keeping you
   from accomplishing a goal.

5} Pick up a book of matches.

6} Set the piece of paper on fire.

7} Throw the burning paper into the toilet.

8} Flush the toilet.

9} Repeat steps 4-8 to rid yourself of obstacles so you can
   feel better and get on with your life.

*Hint: While doing this exercise it helps to sing the simple, three-
word song, "Burn! Throw! Flush!"*

What a great dancer you are.

Realizing Potential

Write down three things that you know you do well. Come on, you can think of three. It could be that you can gift wrap neatly. Or that you always manage to get yourself upgraded at the airport. Or that you *really know* how to give advice without being asked. See, it's simple!

1 } ———————————————————————————————

2 } ———————————————————————————————

3 } ———————————————————————————————

Feeding the Ego

Say hello to 10 people today. You'll find that they happily acknowledge your existence by saying hello, which means they like you. It's easy! Now, go ahead and take the next step and ask them if they like you. We bet they'll say yes!

Hint: Ask people whom you're sure will give you a positive response, like your hairdresser. Because it's best to practice this exercise at places where you spend a lot of money.

People want to feel your magic.

Valuing Your Spirit

Access your personal power and people will want you. Here's a simple way to do that. We call it Teepee Time. Visualize a teepee, or better yet, make one in your living room using a blanket and an umbrella. Sit in your teepee. Don't let anyone else in. This is YOUR teepee! Now close your eyes and soak up the delicious solitude as you revisit You. You'll begin to feel how great you are. Soon others will want to feel you, too!

You are very good-looking.

Redirecting Negativity

Stop the madness. When you are confronted with the nasty voices in your head, channel that noise into a single voice—call it Mr. Negative. Now that you know whom you're talking to, answer these three questions:

1} Why is he *here?*

2} What is he *saying?*

3} How is he *dressed?*

We ask question number three because you'll notice he usually dresses badly, like your ex-boss. Luckily, this automatically negates anything he says to you, because who can take a poor dresser seriously?

Get a Mirror

You are easy to love.

Celebrating You

Love yourself so others can love you. Welcome to The You Game!
It's time to think about YOU! You, you, *you*! What are you doing?
Where are you going? What do you want? This is our favorite
game! We play it all the time. Because in The You Game, you
win! And you can play it anywhere. Just visualize *you* doing your
favorite thing, but *only* you! No one else can be in the picture.
If others start crawling in, just fuzz them out. After all, *you* are
your own best lover.

You are a positive individual.

Embracing Fear

Respond to challenges through action. For example, if someone is not treating you well, type that person a letter. Don't sign it. Explain all the reasons you feel you are being mistreated but don't be so detailed that the person can figure out who you are. Don't put a return address on the envelope. And drive to another town to mail it. This exercise is great because you get to tell people what you're feeling without *really* telling them what you're feeling. And by sending the negativity off in another direction, you're giving yourself a present of positivity!

Finding Outlets

Give your voice an identity. Create your own automated voicemail phone system {but don't bother buying or actually recording anything}. When you answer the phone, just pretend you're an automated message. Greet the caller and then offer a variety of numeric options to press for leaving a message, hearing the weather forecast, or anything else you want. For fun, you can invent different special effects for each option they choose, or sing into the phone if you think someone needs to be put on hold. This will be an exciting new way for you to communicate with the outside world on *your* terms—even though they don't know it.

Letting Love In

Think of yourself as the caretaker of your very own relationship garden. As caretaker, you can manage your relationships in a nurturing, healthy way:

1} Buy some flower seeds, soil and pots.

2} Plant the flower seeds {this can be done in a garden or anywhere else you want to put them}.

3} Give each flower a person's name.

4} Water and talk to your plants as if they were the people in your life.

Now watch your plants as they blossom and grow. You'll realize their true beauty is that they don't demand much of you and they don't talk back.

You don't have a problem.

Selecting Clarity

Identifying a problem is the first step towards solving it.
Condense a problem you're having into one word, like
"Intimacy" or "Jerk." Write it down. Stare at it. Keep staring
at it until your eyes get blurry. After a while, doesn't it start
looking like a foreign word from another language? A
language you've never bothered to learn? Now you know
why you can't resolve your problem. Because you don't have
a problem — you have a language barrier! So go ahead and
name that problem {or the person who has the real prob-
lem} because it's time it starts speaking your language.

Igniting Courage

Tape yourself to a chair. Start with your ankles, then your middle, and finish off by taping your wrists. Any tape will do since this is mainly for mental effect. Then flip yourself over and roll around on the floor screaming as if you've been kidnapped. After an hour or so, remove the tape and jump up and down to celebrate your harrowing escape. You can even pretend to call someone to tell them how you barely freed yourself from danger. You'll notice how alert and prepared you feel after this experience. In fact, you're ready for anything that comes your way — even telemarketers.

Get a Sense of Humor

You generate your own solutions.

Seeing What Is

Get lost. *Really*. Get in your car, start driving, and don't pay attention to where you're going. But make sure to bring a map. Now that you're officially lost, try to locate yourself on the map. This may be difficult if you don't even know who you are, much less where you are. So, take your time. Once you've found yourself, figure out where you are in relation to where you are going. For extra difficulty, drive and read the map at the same time. People may get angry, but at least you're not talking on a cell phone. By the time you get back home, you'll be amazed at how much you've learned. Like how to read a map.

You are here

Transforming Differences

Study the pictures of your family in a photo album. Instead of looking for the similarities between you and them, seek relief by pointing out the differences. If it helps, you can even think of them as complete strangers. Now you can actually enjoy your time together without any of the usual pressure or fighting that normally occurs. Why would you be upset or burdened by a bunch of people you don't know? Just think of how relaxing it can be to be part of a family that really isn't.

You are always right.

Balancing Intentions

Buy a pair of ear plugs. Keep them in at all times. When people try to convince you that their point of view is better than yours, stare directly into their eyes and nod a lot. This creates the illusion that you are actually listening to them. And more important, you get to walk away satisfied that you are always right. People will even begin to think that you're deeply contemplating their position, and praise you as a thoughtful human being. This exercise can last indefinitely depending on how long you can stand letting other people believe that they're actually right.

Planting Hope

You can't expect to feel like the Best You when you aren't eating like the Best You. You must start looking at food as your friend. This means you must stop torturing your friend by cooking it. You'll have to train yourself to eat everything raw. Yes, raw. This will take some getting used to. So, sit with your food. Talk to it. Then blend it in an industrial-size juicer. Follow the raw routine for a month and see how you feel. You might start receiving anonymous gifts of deodorant and toothpaste since your personal odor will be affected by the purging process. But that's part of healing your body from the outside in. So it's good that you made friends with your food — it may be the only one willing to stand by you . . . for awhile.

Removing the Mask

Everyone has an I-spot—the quality that makes her uniquely interesting. You have an I-spot, even if you don't know what it is. Sometimes you just need to reinvigorate your surroundings to help find it.

1} Make cardboard cutouts of life-size bodies and paste or draw the faces of various celebrities, executives at work, hot neighbors, or anyone else who interests you.

2} Place them around your living room and pretend that you are having a cocktail party and these are the people who showed up just to be with you.

3} As the host, go around and role-play the different conversations you would have if these people were actually there. You'll be surprised at the numerous funny comments, delightful insights and clever retorts you can dish out. See how interesting you are? You've just nailed your I-spot!

Recognizing Yourself

It's not always easy to know yourself, especially when you're stuck in a rut. To recall your identity, try on different personalities. Here's the order we suggest:

1} Anal Retentive Control Freak
2} Overly Medicated Optimist
3} Spiritually Depleted Materialist
4} Mind-Numbing Rationalist
5} Happy Confident Normalist

End with Personality #5 to wipe the slate clean before you return to your own personality. In some instances, #1-4 can create strange side effects, such as making excuses for everything and purposely sabotaging relationships. We assure you, after doing this exercise you'll be glad to be back to being you!

Overcoming Challenges

Make your workplace work for you. Reach out to the people you work with by using food as a technique for relating. Visualize something you have in common with everybody. Ice cream, for instance. Everyone likes ice cream. Bring a gallon to the office to share. You'll notice how much easier it is to persuade people when you're all eating. You can practice this exercise using any food item for any job-related situation such as:

1} Asking your boss for a raise:
   "Thought you'd enjoy a little meatloaf . . . . "
2} Making a presentation:
   "Had some extra blueberry pies . . . . "
3} Vying for a project:
   "Knew you'd like my fudge . . . . "

Sometimes a good recipe is all you really need.

Get a Dog or a Baby

{no, just kidding}

❧ ❧

You make choices.

Finding Motivation

Stage a taste test. Go out and buy a lot of different cheeses.
Bring them home and unwrap them, placing each on its
own dish. To make the test more official, put on a chef's hat
and apron and invite friends over. Sample each type of
cheese and decide which one you like best. Now we will
tell you the best part. You've already succeeded in this exercise by buying the cheeses. You were the one who decided
which cheeses to purchase in the first place! Give yourself
credit for being an active participant who knows how to
make choices. Even though you might feel bloated {cheese
tends to do that}.

Relinquishing Needs

Pack for a year-long trip where you can only bring one small bag {it doesn't matter if you actually go anywhere}. Now study your gathering of possessions. We call this the small abyss. Feelings of emptiness and fear may overwhelm you at first as you stare at your little pile, especially if you're used to the comfort of owning a lot of things. But try to remain calm. You might even go into withdrawal and start feeling light-headed. Welcome to material freedom! Let yourself adjust to this powerful new sensation. Soon you'll begin to see that the only possession you need is you. {And of course, money}.

Visualizing Reality

Buy some green construction paper and cut out rectangles in the shape of dollar bills. Then have passport-size photos of yourself made and paste them in the center of the paper. Now add whatever dollar amounts you want to them: $100, $500 — you decide. Surround yourself with your new money. Let your new money sink into your dreams by taping a piece to your forehead before going to bed at night. Stash the new money in various places, like your wallet, pillow, and underwear {it's most effective if you are wearing your underwear at the same time}. Feel the confidence that your new money brings you by pretending to have something you always wanted. Or, just feel happy something is in your pants.

Changing Choices

Claim back a healthier, happier you by letting *go,* especially of anger. Daily nuisances will remain, such as bad drivers, irritating sales help, or people who don't do what you tell them to do. But you do have the power to change how things affect you. For example, when you're driving and someone cuts you off, exclaim how much you like her hair from behind. Or remark on what a beautiful color his car is. Your stress level will immediately decrease and you'll find yourself able to cope with everyday life in a way you never thought possible. It's called survival enlightenment {or, not caring anymore}.

Validating Possibility

If you don't like the world you're in, make one up by building your own universe in your bedroom. Buy glow-in-the-dark planets and stars, and stick them on your ceiling. You can add extra little details by making galaxies out of wire, cotton and tin foil. Then take a pen and draw your ideal existence. Name planets after the types of people you want to have in your life. Label the stars with the character traits you wish you had. And, for the best of all possible worlds, assign to each galaxy one of the hundreds of goals you want to achieve without having to work for them. Now, whenever you need to visualize your perfect life, just turn off the lights, stand back, and feel the glory of being the creator of your own universe.

Obtaining Self-Reliance

Seize your own opportunity for greatness by believing in yourself. Create your own superhero costume. Think updated leisure suit but with lots of glitter, feathers, and super glue. Then take a permanent marker and write your favorite action word on the front of the costume. Choose a word that inspires you, like "caffeine." Now, dress up in your hero outfit whenever you're feeling down or doubtful. As you wear it, you'll begin to exude a newfound strength. In fact, you'll feel so confident you may never want to wear anything else again. Which is great since you'll find being a hero never goes out of style!

Hair Mantra

I l-o-v-e   my   hair   which makes me   successful at   l - i - f - e
since   I've real-l-y got it   to   gether   soooooooooo
everything   I say is   fas-cin-ating____
because
there's   just   something special   about   M-E!
therefore   my   perception of reality is right on target
because
I   loooooook attractive in any   thing I wear so-o-o
I   make   things   happen   which means   that
I'm a g-r-e-a-t dancer   and people real-l-y like M-E!
so they want to feel my magic…after all,
I am very good looking
which
makes me   easy to l-o-v-e____
and a pos-i-tive in-di-vid-u-al
who can express her   self
so-o-oo-ooo____
I don't   have   a   prob   lem because
I kn-o-w
what to do in a crisis by gen-er-a-ting
my o w n solutions
which means I enjo-o-oy the holidays____
be   cause   I   am
al-ways right and I eat well bal-anced meals
which   makes   me so-o-o much m-o-r-e interesting than mo-o-st people
be-cause____
I know who I am,
I   even   like my job   and   I am able to make choices
so that I can pack for travel since
I   know   ho-o-ow to let go
while making a l o t of   money   b-y
creating my own des-tin-y
be-cause   I   am   m-y   own   her-o.